THE UGLY DUCKLING

THE UGLY DUCKLING

It was summer in the countryside and the weather was lovely. At the foot of an old castle, near a deep moat surrounded by thick bushes, a mother duck had made her nest and was waiting for her eggs to hatch. She was bored since she had no one to talk to and impatient to see her little ducklings.

Suddenly, she heard the crack! crack! crack! of the eggs as they began to open one after another. The little ducklings came out head first, marveling as they looked around at the grass and flowers. There hadn't been much to see when they were cooped up in their shells.

"Children, this is just a tiny bit of the big wonderful world that stretches out far beyond the woods and fields," said the mother duck. "Now let me count and see how many of you I have."

"Oh dear," said the duck as she got off the nest. "The biggest egg hasn't hatched yet. I'd better keep sitting on it." After what seemed like forever, the big egg finally cracked open. "Peep! Peep!" said the little duckling

as he rolled out onto the grass. The mother duck stared at her newest arrival in disbelief. He was big and very ugly indeed. “He doesn’t look at all like his brothers and sisters,” she thought.

The next day, the weather was fine so the mother duck took her brood down to the water’s edge. She jumped in and quacked to her children to join her. The little ducklings all leapt in, one after another, even the big, ugly one. They dove under the water, bobbed back up and swam beautifully, paddling with their little webbed feet. The grey duckling swam just as well as the others, a big smile on his face.

“Look at how well he can swim!” said the mother. “He’s definitely my son. And he’s not that homely when you take a closer look at him. Come children. I’m going to introduce you to the barnyard folk. Stay close to me all the time so you don’t get stepped upon.”

As they approached the barnyard, they heard a terrible racket. There were already several duck families there. The young ducks teased and pecked at each other while the parents tried to restore order. “Please, try to get along among yourselves and with the other ducks,” begged the mother duck.

But the other ducks stared at the new arrivals and said, "Well, well, well, looks like we're going to have yet another family. As if there weren't enough of us here already." "Look at that one!" said one of the ducks. "He's really hideous. What a face!"

"Get this freak out of here," said another.

"Let's chase him away," cried a third, biting the duckling on the neck.

"Leave him alone," said the mother. "He hasn't done you any harm."

"He's way too big and looks ridiculous," replied the duck. "He deserves a thrashing!"

Just then, the wisest and oldest duck in the barnyard came over to see what was going on. "Listen, we all know the barnyard should be a peaceful place." She turned to the mother duck and said, "You have lovely children, my dear, except for that one (pointing at the ugly duckling). Too bad you can't trade him for a nicer one."

"Well, that's not possible," replied the mother duck. "He may not be handsome, but he's smart and swims just as well as the others. I hope that with time he will become more beautiful and everyone can appreciate how kind he is." She smoothed her feathers with her beak to make herself look

more dignified. “Besides, he is my son and I will not tolerate anyone hurting him.”

“Very well,” said the wise old duck. “I hope you're right and that he improves as he grows older. In the meantime, you and your family are welcome to stay here.”

But the poor duckling was so huge and clumsy that he became the laughing-stock of the barnyard. The ducks, the hens and even the turkeys bossed him around and pecked at him. The poor creature no longer knew where to hide. He had so many enemies that even his mother could not defend him.

Early one morning, the guard dog chased him out of the yard. The duckling took flight to escape the dog's jaws. He was so frightened that he flew for a long time. He flew over fields and forests and landed in a marsh he had never seen before. He could not even remember how he had gotten there. He was lost.

The dark, gloomy marsh was full of scary noises, so he decided that he would leave to search for shelter elsewhere. He walked across the fields until, late at night, he reached a humble cottage. He managed to slip inside through a space between two boards.

The cottage was home to an old peasant woman, her hen and her tomcat. The hen was a good layer even though she had short, stumpy legs. The cat could purr beautifully and arch his back gracefully. In the morning, the entire household stared at the stranger. The cat meowed and the hen went, “Cluck, cluck, cluck!”

“What have we here?” said the old woman, whose eyesight was no longer very sharp. “Why, it looks like a big duck, who can lay delicious eggs for us. Come here, my dear, don’t be afraid. We’ll give you shelter and you show us what you can do.”

She had mistaken the duckling for a female. He accepted the offer to stay but it soon became obvious that he was not about to lay any eggs.

The hen and the cat thought they were very smart and did not like being contradicted. “Can you lay eggs?” asked the hen.

“No,” said the duckling.

“Well then, shut up,” she said scornfully.

And the cat said, “Can you arch your back and purr?”

“Of course not,” replied the duckling.

"Well, then, you have nothing to say," hissed the cat.

The duckling felt frustrated. He yearned to be free and foolishly shared his feelings with the hen.

"You know what's wrong with you? You don't know how to do anything," said the hen. "That's why you're so miserable. Just learn to lay eggs or purr and you'll feel much better."

"But it's so wonderful to fly freely about," said the duckling. "I just love to swim in the pond, dive to the bottom and bob back up!"

"That sounds just ducky," smirked the hen. "You really are daft. Ask the cat. He's the next smartest creature on the earth, after me. Ask him if he wants to glide around on the water or dive to the bottom of a pond. Do you think he wants to get all wet?"

"You just don't understand," sighed the duckling.

"Is that so? And if we don't understand you, then who will? Do you think you are smarter than the cat or me? Don't be such a ninny! You should thank heaven for what you have here. A warm home and friends who can teach you a thing or two. You're just a big good-for-nothing!"

"I really feel hurt and misunderstood," replied the duckling. "I think the big, wide world can teach me more than a cat or hen ever could. And I intend to find out."

"Well, go right ahead then," chuckled the hen. "Scram!"

And so the duckling did just that. He swam, dove beneath the water and leapt into the air. But wherever he went, all the animals that saw him were repulsed by his ugliness and did not understand his love of freedom.

Fall came, and then winter. The duckling travelled from pond to pond, vainly searching for happiness. The weather was bitterly cold and he had to swim constantly to keep the water from freezing up around him. But the hole in the ice got smaller and smaller as the days went by. The ice, the snow and the harsh cold threatened to make him a prisoner there forever.

Yet, slowly but surely, the sun grew warmer and the days grew longer. The larks sang as spring arrived. The duckling tried his wings and took flight with a new strength and an energy he had never dreamed possible. He soon found himself in a garden filled with blooming apple trees and fragrant lilac bushes.

As he looked up, he saw three magnificent white swans land gracefully on the pond. They swam regally toward him, their beautiful wings curved behind them. The duckling had never seen such stunning creatures before. He felt his heart leap as he approached them shyly.

"Greetings," said the duckling. "I am surely not worthy of speaking to such majestic creatures, but I feel I absolutely must."

"What are you saying?" asked one of the swans. "Are you making fun of us or do you really not know what you are?"

"I would never dare make fun of you," replied the duckling. "I would rather sink to the bottom of the pond than remain an ugly duckling for the rest of my life."

Hearing his reply, the swans burst into laughter, because they had already heard the sad tale of the ugly duckling.

"Come, my friend," said the swan. "Take a good look at your reflection and tell me what you see."

The duckling looked down at the water's surface and saw an amazing thing. What he saw there was not a big, ugly grey bird. To his astonishment, he saw that he had become a swan! He wept with delight at his discovery.

His friends smiled as they watched him. “Yes, you’re just like us,” they said.

The duckling felt such joy, as if all his suffering had finally been rewarded. And then he felt a sudden urge to see his mother again. So he spread his majestic white wings and flew over the marshes, forests and fields, back to where he was born. He greeted his mother, who recognized him immediately, despite his new appearance. They spent many long and happy hours together, walking and talking. All the ducks in the barnyard bowed their heads before the magnificent swan in their midst. “I have found happiness at long last,” said the swan. “And now I want to teach the barnyard folk that they must respect all creatures, even those who seem different from the rest.”